Kumon Creative Doodling Workbooks

My Amazing
Doodle & Draw Workbook

Parent's Guide

This book uses a carefully structured, step-by-step approach that allows your child to have fun and build confidence while developing creativity and problem-solving skills. To help your child get the maximum benefit from this book, we recommend the following:

- Have your child start at the beginning of the book and complete the activities in order, rather than skipping around.
- Encourage your child to have fun. Let him or her know that there is no single correct response.
- Allow your child to draw things from his or her imagination as well as real-life things and events.
- Refer to the sample responses on page 128 if your child needs additional guidance.
- Limit the number of pages your child completes in a day so he or she still wants to do a little more at the end of each session.

The "To parents" notes throughout this book provide more comments and advice on how to support your child as he or she completes the activities.

You will notice that the activities in this book become more challenging as your child progresses through them. A primary goal of the book is to prepare your child to complete the problem-solving activities at the end of the book. The activities in the book are grouped in the following six sections:

(1) Coloring: The coloring tasks help build confidence and introduce your child to the format of the book. To begin, your child will use only one designated color. As your child progresses through this section, he or she will use more colors and also make his or her own color choices.

(2) Decorating: The decorating tasks involve drawing patterns. To begin, your child will copy one pattern shown in the picture. As your child progresses, he or she can choose from various patterns to copy and also design his or her own patterns.

(3) Drawing Something Specific: In these activities, your child will add something to the picture. The directions give specific information about what to add. To begin, your child can copy examples shown in the picture. Later on, the activities encourage your child to exercise more creativity in choosing what to draw and how to draw it.

(4) Drawing with Shapes: In these activities, your child will turn shapes into a variety of different objects. As your child progresses through the section, he or she will exercise more creativity in choosing what to draw and how to draw it.

(5) Drawing Something Creative: These activities require more creativity and decision-making ability than the previous tasks. Your child will decide what to add to each picture with little direction from the instructions. It is important for your child to recognize that there is no single correct response for each task.

(6) Problem Solving: In these activities, each picture shows a problem. Your child will add something to the picture to solve the problem. To complete these tasks, your child will draw on the creativity, fine motor skills, and decision-making abilities that he or she has been practicing throughout the book.

Coloring
Rabbits in the Garden

■ Color the carrots.

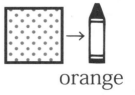

orange

Bobtail

Coloring
Chicks Hatching

■ Color the chicks.

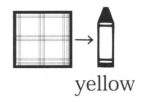

yellow

To parents: The first coloring activities in this book use only one color. This beginning-level task helps to build your child's confidence and familiarity with the book.

5

Coloring
Making Burgers

■ Color the ketchup.

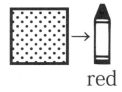

red

To parents: Many children enjoy pretending to cook. With this activity your child can pretend to be making burgers.

American Shorthair

Coloring
Fruit Bowl

■ Color the grapes and strawberries.

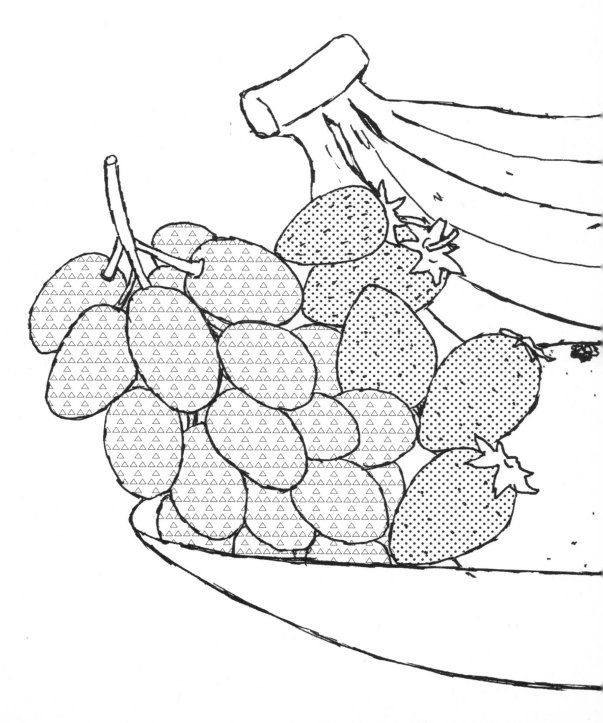

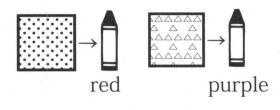

red   purple

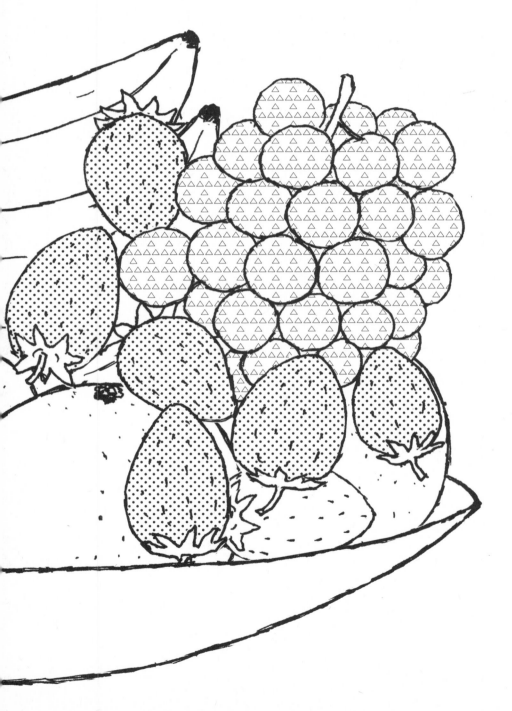

Coloring
Busy Street

■ Color the fire trucks and taxis.

red   yellow

To parents: You may wish to help your child locate the fire trucks and taxis in the picture.

Coloring
On the Loose

The animals are loose at the zoo! Color the flamingos and bears.

Exotic
Shorthair

pink   brown

13

Coloring
Stunning Snake

Color the hearts and diamonds.

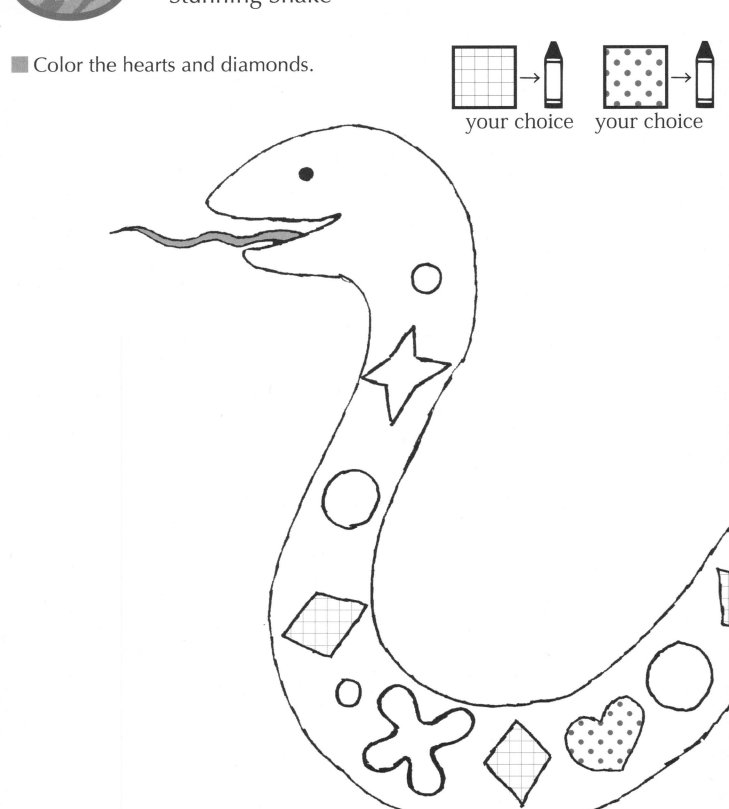

your choice   your choice

Aegean

Coloring
Lightning Strikes

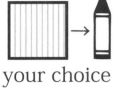
your choice

■ Color the lightning.

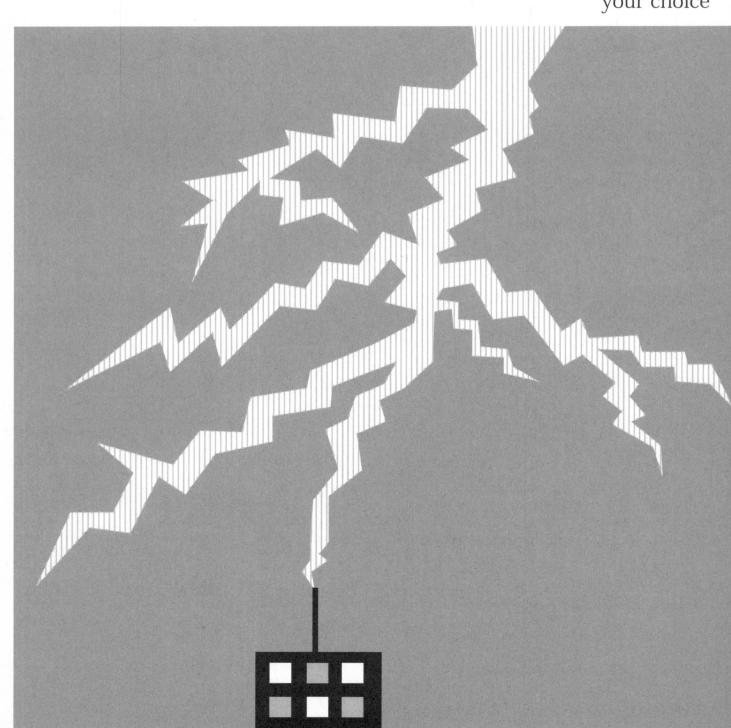

Siamese

9 Coloring
All Dressed Up

Color our ties.

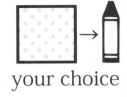

your choice

To parents: Your child can use the same color for all four ties or different colors.

19

Coloring
Trains Through a Tunnel

■ Color the trains.

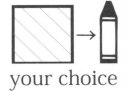

your choice

Ocicat

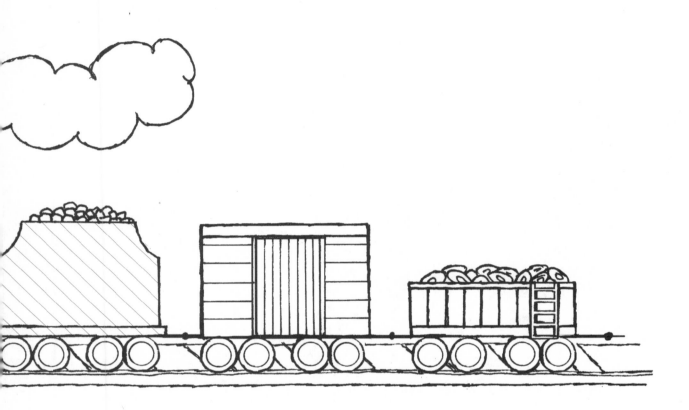

Decorating
Missing Stripes

One of the zebras is missing some stripes. Can you help?

Cymric

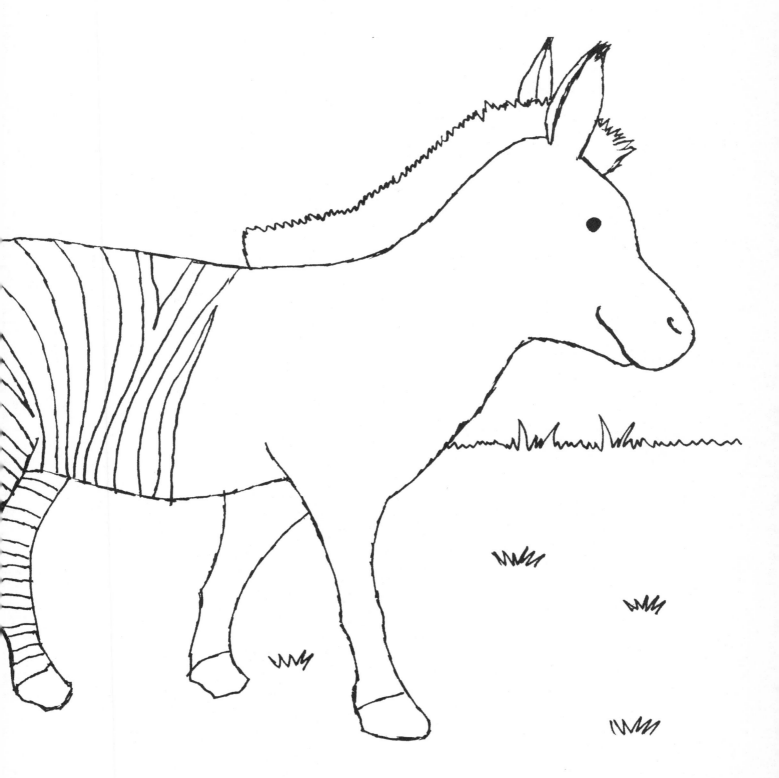

Decorating
Missing Spots

■ Some of the ladybugs are missing their spots. Can you add them?

To parents: Encourage your child to look at the spots on the other ladybugs before he or she begins drawing.

Decorating
Waves on Vases

Can you decorate the last vase?

To parents: If your child has difficulty, ask him or her to describe the pattern on the other vases.

Decorating
Spotted Suitcase

Decorate my suitcase. Be sure to use my favorite pattern!

To parents: Ask your child what pattern he or she sees on the woman's clothing.

Siberian

Decorating
Lovely Lizards

One of the lizards is missing a pattern. Can you decorate it?

To parents: Starting with this activity, there are several different patterns shown in the picture. Your child can choose from the patterns shown or draw other patterns.

Japanese Bobtail

31

Decorating
Laundry Day

■ Decorate the T-shirt and shorts.

To parents: Your child can use the same pattern on the T-shirt and shorts or two different patterns.

Decorating
Creative Cakes

Help me decorate the last cake.

Decorating
Fabulous Feet

■ Decorate our socks.

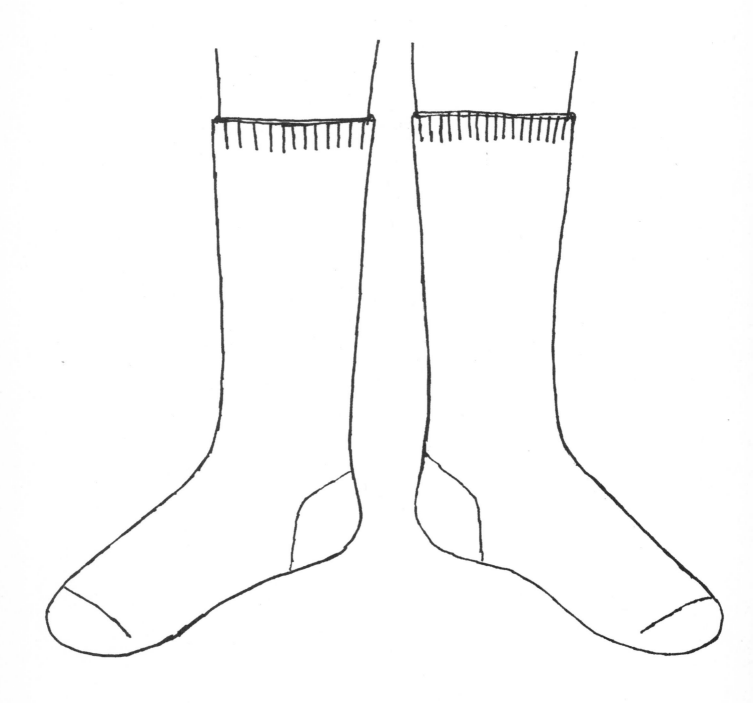

Scottish Fold

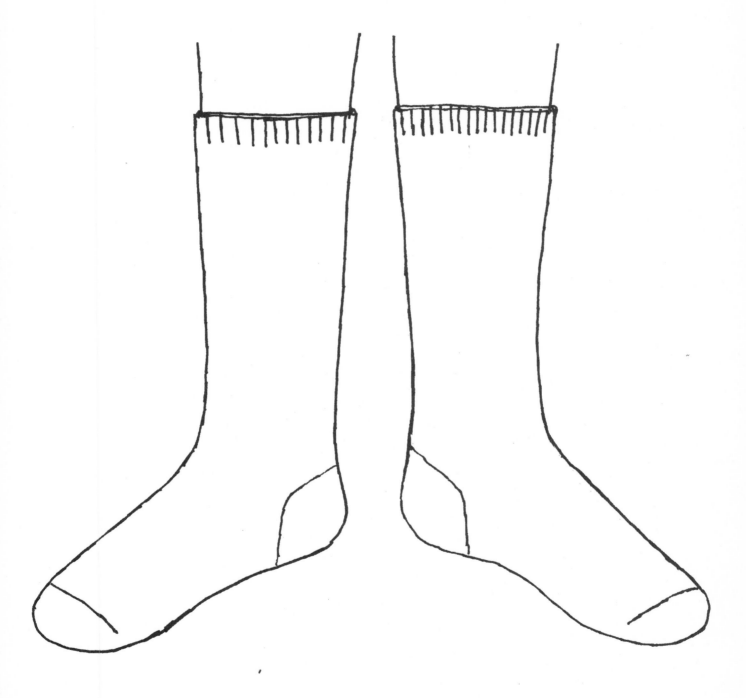

Decorating
Wonderful Wings

Decorate our wings.

Snowshoe

Decorating
Pretty Parasols

Please decorate our beautiful parasols.

Kurilian
Bobtail

21 Drawing Something Specific
In the Jungle

Draw more vines for the monkeys to swing on.

Selkirk
Rex

Drawing Something Specific
Snowball Fight

■ Draw more snowballs.

Somali

Drawing Something Specific
Feed the Dolphins

Help throw the dolphins some yummy fish.

Turkish Angora

Drawing Something Specific
Ants Underground

■ Draw more ants in the tunnels.

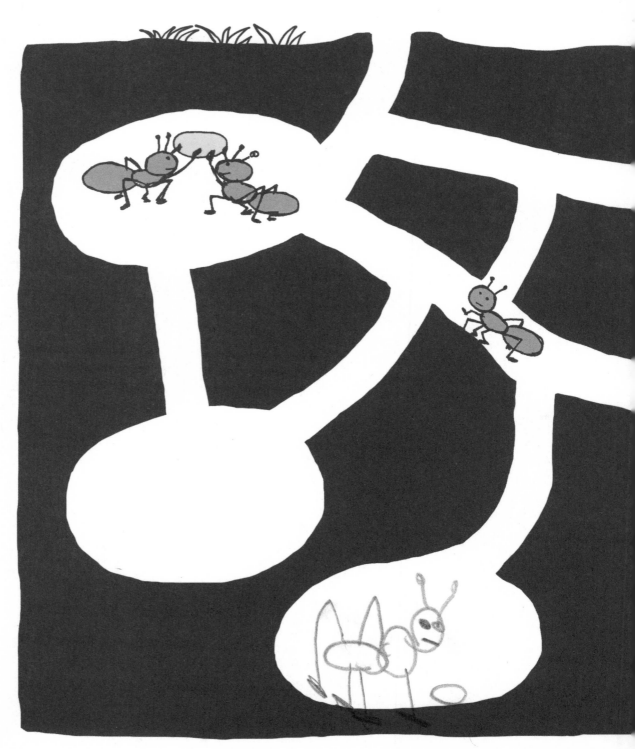

Drawing Something Specific
Ice Cream Parlor

■ We need one more ice cream sundae, fast! Can you make it?

Drawing Something Specific
Inspecting Insects

■ What did I catch inside my net?

Norwegian Forest

Drawing Something Specific
Time to Swing

■ Can you draw some swings for us?

Pixie-bob

Drawing Something Specific
Game of Hoops

◼ Where's the basketball?

29 Drawing Something Specific
Around the Campfire

■ Can you light the campfire?

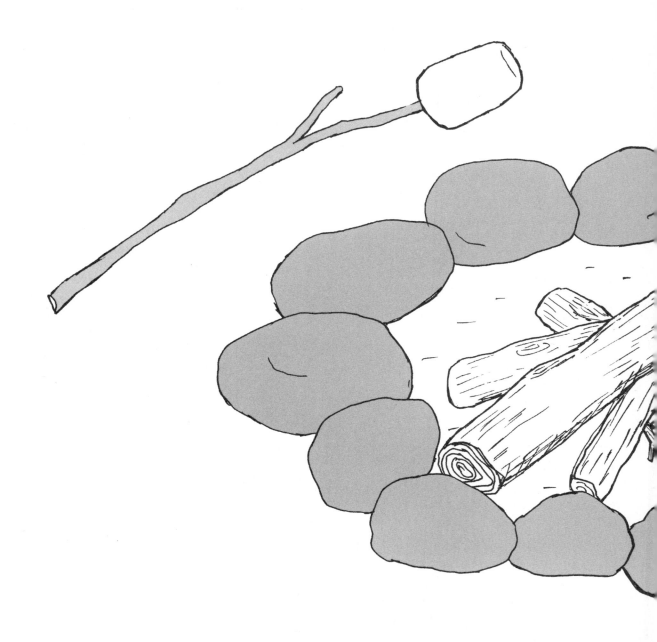

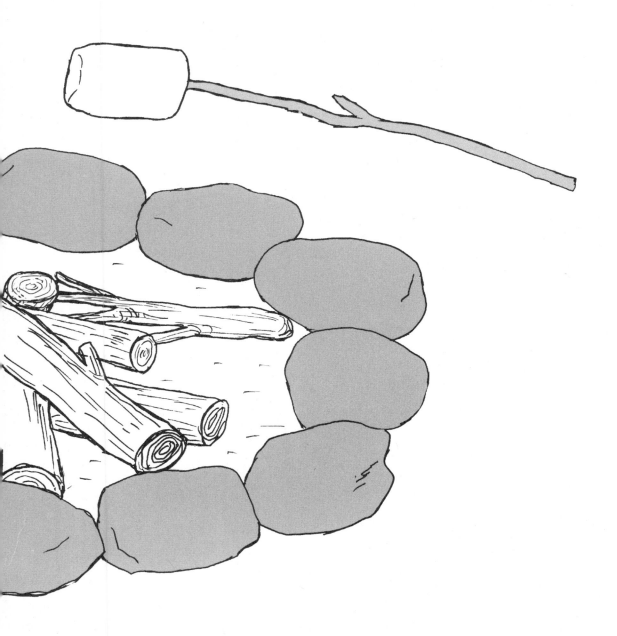

Drawing Something Specific
Wild Waterslide

■ Draw a crazy waterslide into the pool.

To parents: This is the last activity in this section. The directions provide specific instructions about what to draw, but they also leave a lot of room for creativity. Encourage your child to have fun.

Drawing with Shapes
Juicy Fruits

■ Turn these circles into an apple and an orange.

Drawing with Shapes
Off to School

■ Turn this shape into a school bus.

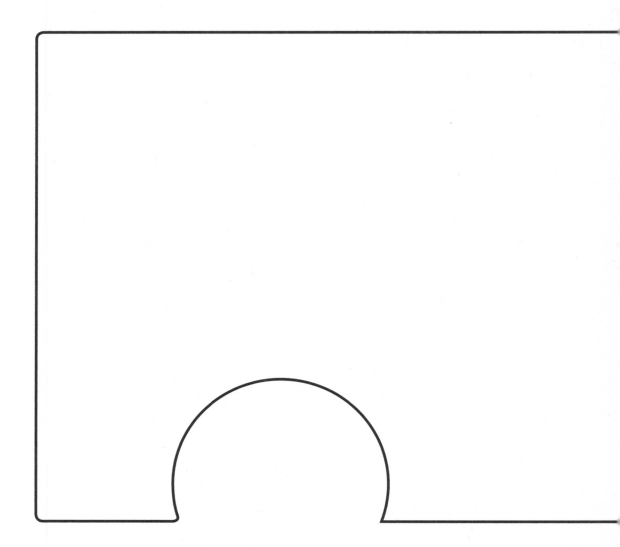

To parents: If your child has difficulty, have him or her point to the part of the shape that looks like the front of a bus.

Manx

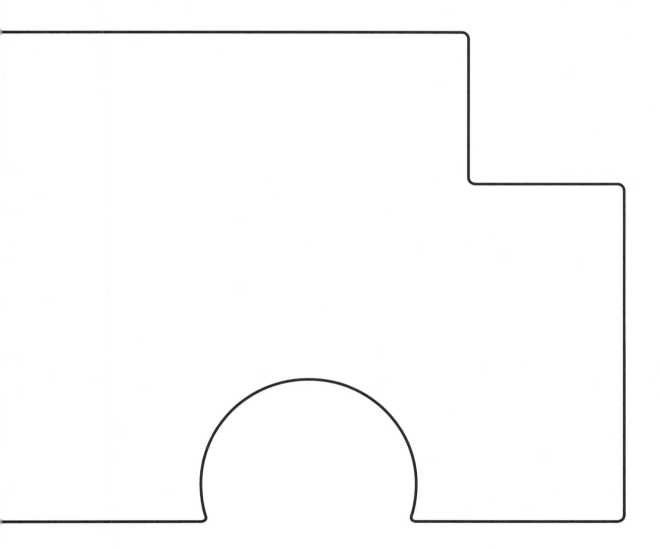

Drawing with Shapes
Light the Candles

■ Turn these shapes into candles.

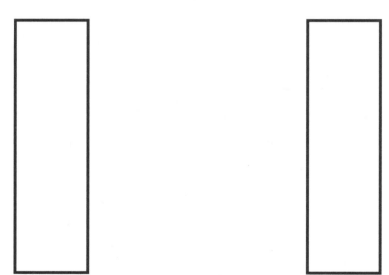

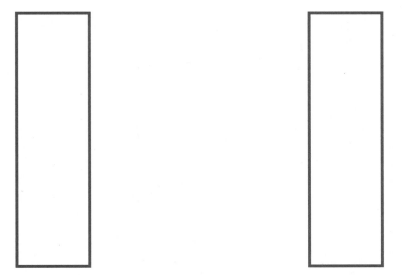

34 Drawing with Shapes
Go Fly a Kite

■ Turn these shapes into kites.

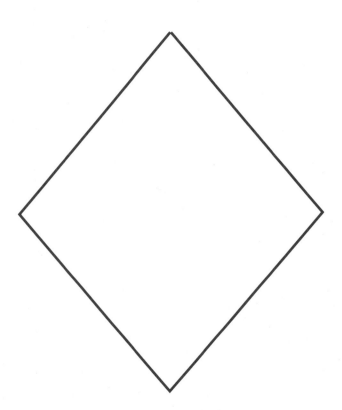

To parents: **If your child has difficulty, talk together about the different parts of a kite.**

Maine
Coon

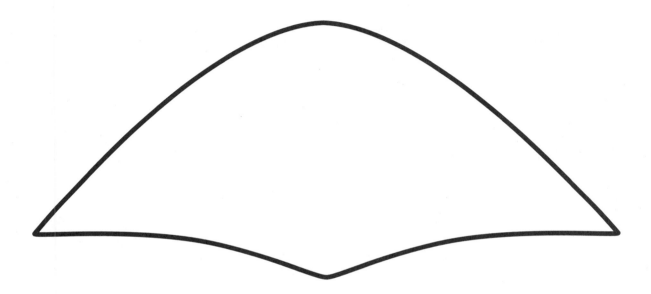

■ Turn this shape into a turtle.

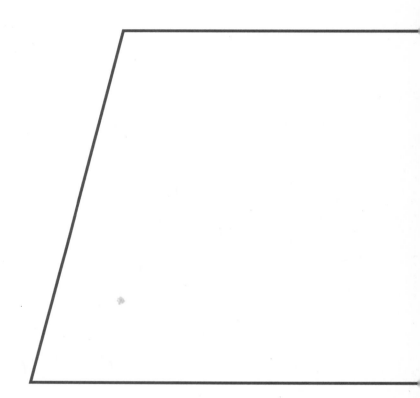

Drawing with Shapes
Terrific Teeth

■ Turn these shapes into teeth inside a mouth.

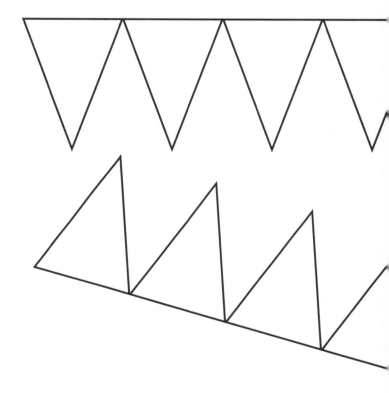

To parents: For an added challenge, encourage your child to think of a few different ways of creating his or her drawing, before getting started.

Ragdoll

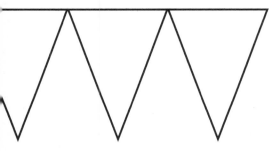

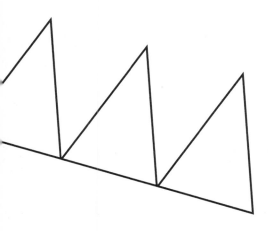

Drawing with Shapes
Wondrous Windows

Turn these shapes into windows.

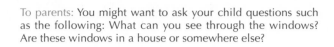

Drawing with Shapes
Very Hairy

■ Turn these shapes into hair.

Russian
Blue

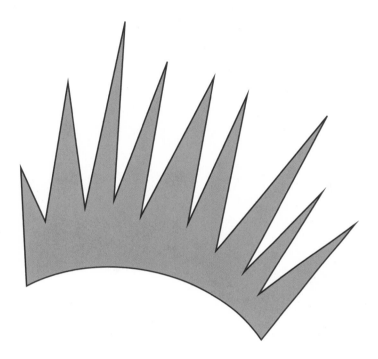

Drawing with Shapes
Rectangles Rule

■ Turn these shapes into anything you want.

Drawing with Shapes
Two Tubes

■ Turn these shapes into anything you want.

To parents: Encourage your child to talk about what he or she wants to draw, before getting started.

Serengeti

Drawing Something Creative
Time to Eat

■ What's cooking?

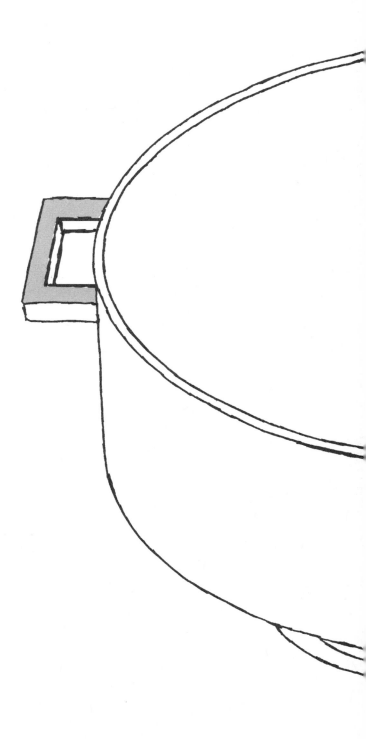

Sokoke

42 Drawing Something Creative
A Present for You

■ What's in the box?

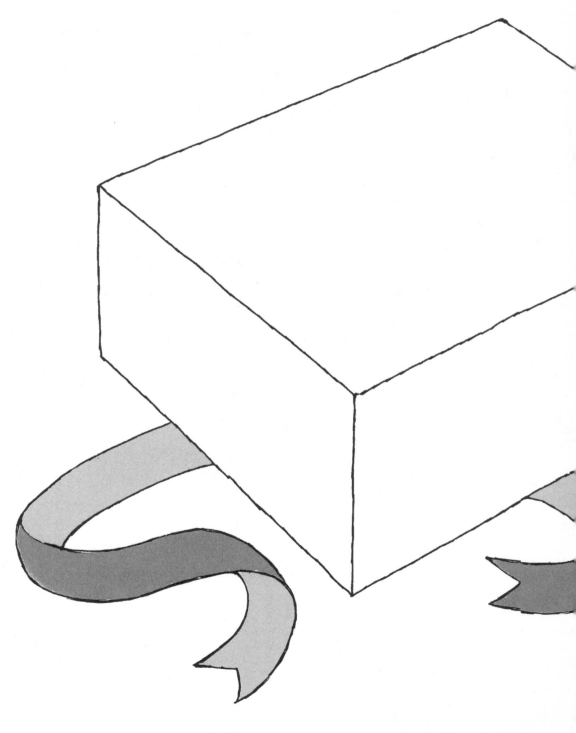

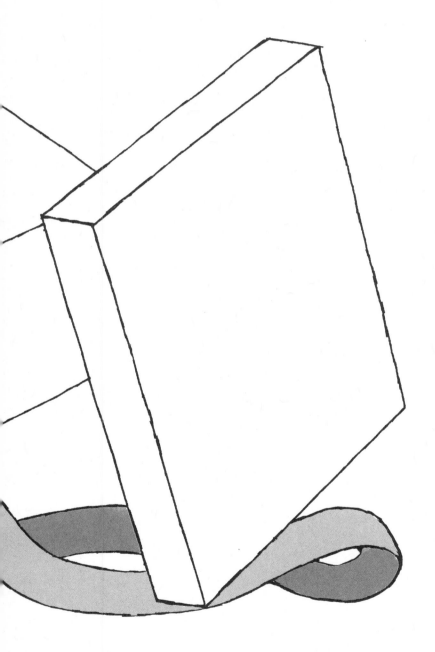

Drawing Something Creative
At the Store

■ What's in my grocery cart?

To parents: You might want to encourage your child to draw his or her favorite foods in the grocery cart.

Chausie

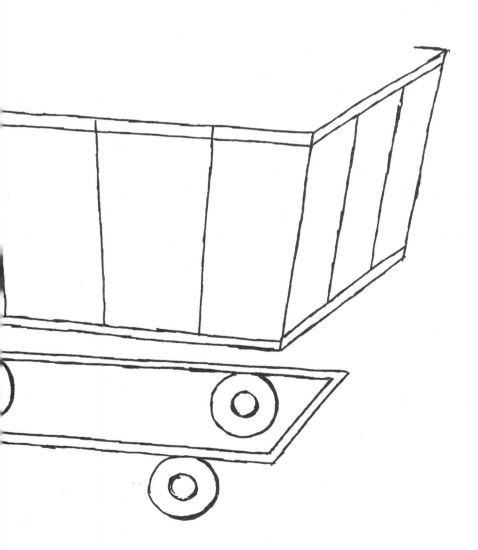

Drawing Something Creative
Stuck in a Tree

■ Who or what is stuck in the tree?

Arabian Mau

Drawing Something Creative
Race to the Finish

■ Draw the contestants in the race. Who is winning?

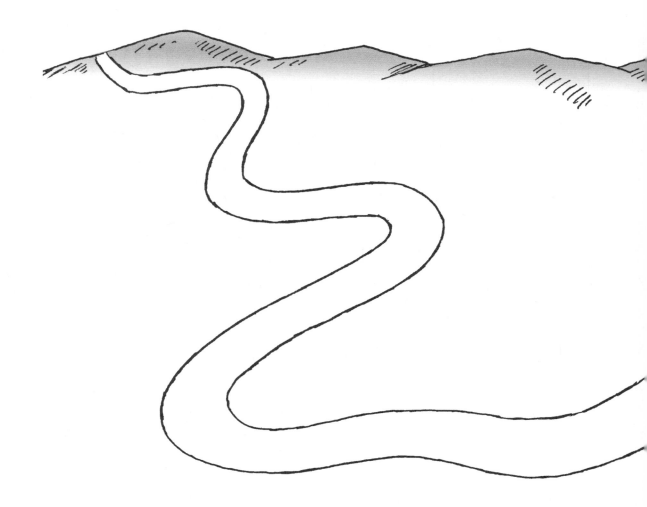

46 Drawing Something Creative
Hanging On

■ What are we hanging on to?

To parents: If your child has difficulty, help your child brainstorm ideas or refer to page 128.

Asian
Semi-
longhair

Drawing Something Creative
An Underwater Adventure

■ What do the scuba divers see?

Ojos
Azules

Drawing Something Creative
Look Out Below

■ Where will I land?

To parents: If your child has difficulty, encourage him or her to draw something near the bottom of one or both pages, where the parachuter is likely to land.

49 Drawing Something Creative
Space Adventure

■ Where is this spaceship headed?

Colorpoint
Shorthair

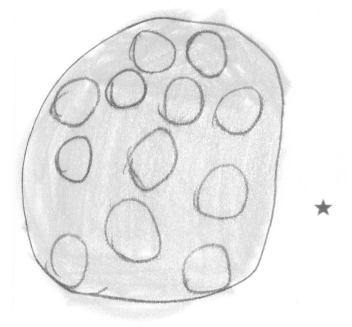

50 Drawing Something Creative
Dinosaur's Pet

■ What's at the end of the leash?

Semi-
cobby

Problem Solving
Sail Away

■ Our boat isn't moving! Can you help?

To parents: Starting with this activity, each picture shows a problem. Your child will add something to the picture to solve the problem.

Problem Solving
Floating Away

Some of the balloons are floating away. Can you help?

To parents: If your child has difficulty, point to the balloons in the picture that are not floating away. Ask your child why they do not float away.

Brazilian
Shorthair

Problem Solving
Empty Pool

The diver is about to dive into an empty pool! Can you help?

To parents: Encourage your child to notice what is missing from the pool.

Australian
Mist

Problem Solving
Rainstorm

There's a sudden rainstorm on the way to school! Can you help us stay dry?

Mekong
Bobtail

Problem Solving
Across the Canyon

■ Help me get to the other side.

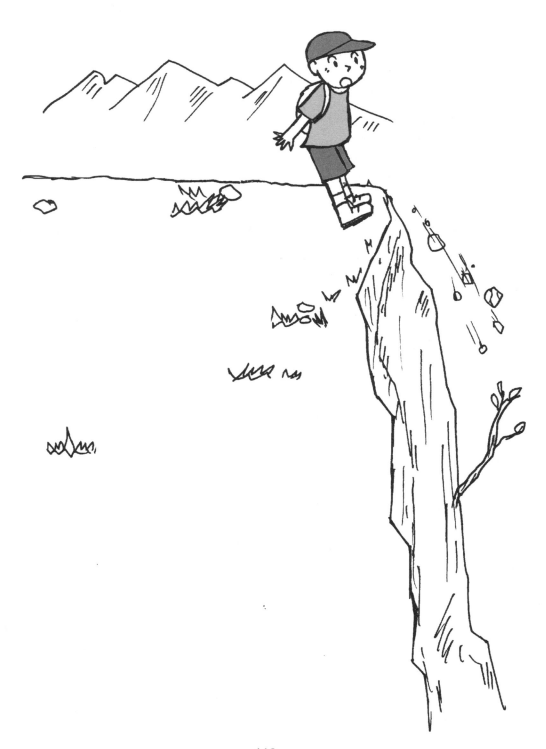

Ukranian
Levkoy

Problem Solving
Island Rescue

Help me get off the island!

Seychellois

57 Problem Solving

Secret Treehouse

■ Help us get into the treehouse.

To parents: You may want to talk with your child about treehouses he or she has seen, either in real life or in pictures, before getting started.

European Shorthair

Problem Solving
Scared Kitten

■ Keep the kitten safe from the dog!

To parents: You may notice that the activities are becoming more challenging as your child progresses through the book. Congratulate your child on his or her hard work so far.

Havana

Problem Solving
Something Fishy

■ Don't let the fish get caught in the net!

To parents: If your child has difficulty, talk about general ways to solve the problem. For example, one approach is to get the fish to swim away from the net.

Dragon Li

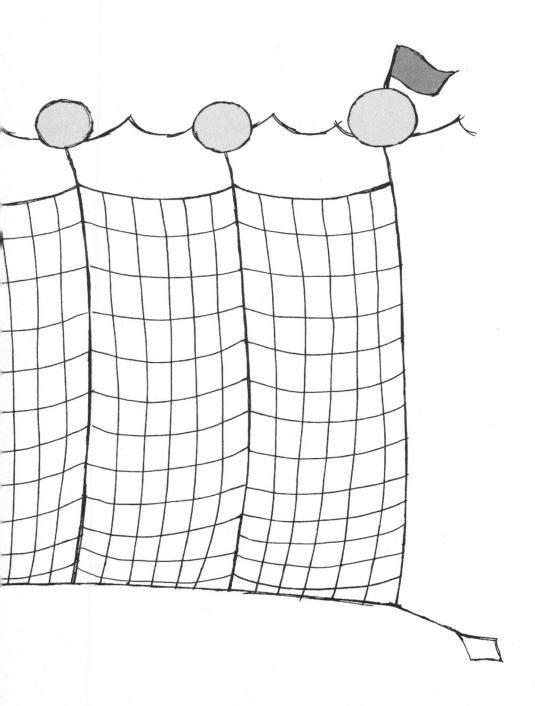

119

Problem Solving
Hard to Stop

Help me stop safely!

Minskin

Problem Solving
Giant Wave

Save my sand castle from the giant wave!

To parents: Remember that your child's drawing does not
need to show something that can happen in real life.

Problem Solving
Falling Rock

■ Save me from the falling rock!

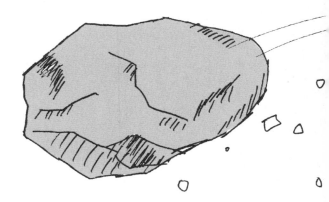

To parents: If your child has difficulty, talk about general ways to solve the problem. For example, one approach is to give the person protection from the falling boulder.

Tiffany

Problem Solving
In the Hole

■ We dropped our toy car into a hole! Help us get it out.

To parents: This is the last activity in the workbook. When your child has finished, offer him or her lots of praise.

Khao Manee

Sample Responses

There are no right or wrong answers for the activities in this book. However, descriptions of sample responses are provided below. These are provided as a guide if your child needs support completing the activities.

1 Color the carrots orange.
2 Color the chicks yellow.
3 Color the ketchup on the hamburgers red.
4 Color the strawberries red and the grapes purple.
5 Color the fire trucks red and the taxis yellow.
6 Color the flamingos pink and the bears brown.
7 Color the hearts any color. Color the diamonds any color.
8 Color the lightning any color or colors.
9 Color the ties any color or colors.
10 Color the train cars any color or colors.
11 Finish drawing stripes on the zebra on the right-hand page.
12 Add any number of dots to the two ladybugs without them.
13 Add a wavy line pattern to the undecorated vase.
14 Add a polka dot pattern to the suitcase.
15 Add a pattern to the lizard in the upper left. Choose from the patterns on the other lizards or develop a new one.
16 Add patterns to the T-shirt and shorts. Choose from the patterns on the other clothing or develop new ones.
17 Decorate the cake on the right-hand page. Choose from the designs shown on the other cakes or develop new ones.
18 Add patterns to the socks. You may wish to create two matching pairs.
19 Decorate the butterflies' wings. Add the same pattern to each butterfly or make each one different.
20 Decorate the parasols. Add the same pattern to each parasol or make each one different.
21 Draw one vine for each monkey that is not holding one.
22 Draw snowballs in the air and add more snowballs to the piles beside each person.
23 Draw more fish in the air above the dolphins. You may want to draw one in a dolphin's mouth.
24 Add three or four more ants crawling through the tunnels.
25 Draw a sundae in the cup on the right-hand page. Copy one of the others shown or combine elements from all three.
26 Draw a butterfly and a dragonfly in the net.
27 Draw three swings, one for each child who is waiting.
28 Draw the basketball right above the hoop, about to fall through the net.
29 Use orange, red, and yellow to make colorful flames.
30 Draw a slide with an upside-down loop, like in a roller coaster.
31 Color one circle red and add a stem and leaf. Color the other circle orange and add dots to show texture.
32 Add two circles for wheels. Add squares for windows and a rectangle for the door.
33 Draw an orange flame on top of each candle. Draw a cupcake underneath each candle.
34 Turn each shape into a kite by adding a kite tail and a line.
35 Draw the turtle's head, legs, and tail along the bottom of the shape.

36 Draw a crocodile's mouth seen from the side or a snarling monster seen from the front.
37 Draw curtains or blinds to partially cover the windows and a landscape visible through each window.
38 Draw two people with spiky hair, one person with hair poking over his or her ears, or two hairy arms reaching out from the page.
39 Draw a brick wall under construction, a child playing with building blocks, or a platform for winners of a race.
40 Draw glasses of lemonade, test tubes in a science lab, or trash cans.
41 Draw hearty stew, warm oatmeal, or bubbling witch's brew.
42 Draw a teddy bear, a book, or a video game in the box.
43 Draw foods such as eggs, milk, bread, bananas, and tomatoes.
44 Draw a cat, a toy airplane, or a child in the tree.
45 Draw two or three runners along the path or characters from the story of the tortoise and the hare.
46 Draw tree branches, trapezes, or a giant kite.
47 Draw a treasure chest, a shipwreck, or a whale.
48 Draw a grassy field, a pond filled with ducks, or the top of a skyscraper.
49 Draw Earth, the moon, or a made-up planet with aliens.
50 Draw a cat, a dog, or a small dinosaur.
51 Draw a sail on the boat.
52 Draw strings on the balloons.
53 Draw water in the pool.
54 Draw umbrellas or raincoats for the children.
55 Draw a bridge across the canyon or a springboard that the boy can use to jump across.
56 Draw a rowboat on the sand, a cruise ship passing nearby, or a helicopter hovering above the island.
57 Draw a wooden ladder, a knotted rope, or a flight of stairs.
58 Draw a fence between the dog and the kitten, or add a leash held by a person or tied to the tree.
59 Draw a shark to scare the fish into swimming in the opposite direction, or draw scissors cutting the ropes that attach the net to the buoys.
60 Draw a platform that extends beyond the edge of the cliff, a bungee cord that will keep the person from skating off the cliff, or a giant pile of soft feathers for the person to land in.
61 Draw a large moat or brick wall between the wave and the sand castle, or draw a giant fan to blow the water in the opposite direction.
62 Draw a steel cage around the boy to protect him from the falling rock, draw a crane supporting the rock so it cannot fall, or draw a garden hose squirting the boy so he moves out of the way of the falling rock.
63 Draw a fishing rod and hook to catch the toy, or water in the hole to float the toy to the surface.